INVESTING IN
INDUSTRIAL
REAL ESTATE

A Practical Guide By A Qualified Attorney

Ronald Rohde, Esq.

Jacobs & Whitehall
73-03 Bell Blvd, #10
Oakland Gardens, NY 11364
(888) 570-7338
www.jacobsandwhitehall.com

Ordering Information:

Quantity sales. Special discounts are available on quantity purchases by corporations, associations, and others. For details, contact the publisher at the address above.

Orders by U.S. trade bookstores and wholesalers. Please contact Jacobs & Whitehall: Tel: (888) 991-2766 or visit www.jacobsandwhitehall.com.

Printed in the United States of America

Published in 2021

ISBN: 978-1-954506-26-8

DISCLAIMER

This publication is intended to be used for educational purposes only. No legal advice is being given, and no attorney-client relationship is intended to be created by reading this material. The author assumes no liability for any errors or omissions or for how this book or its contents are used or interpreted, or for any consequences resulting directly or indirectly from the use of this book. For legal or any other advice, please consult an experienced attorney or the appropriate expert, who is aware of the specific facts of your case and is knowledgeable in the law in your jurisdiction.

Law Office of Ronald Rohde, PLLC
8350 N. Central Expressway Suite 1900
Dallas, Texas 75206
(707) 574 8989
www.ronaldrohdelaw.com

TESTIMONIALS

"I have referred Ron several clients over the years and he has treated them with respect. Many are capable of doing the work you request, but Ron takes it to another level with his due diligence and client-centered focus. Got a business or real estate deal or concern? Ron is the one to call. Thank you Ron."

– John

****

TABLE OF CONTENTS

ABOUT THE AUTHOR

My parents have always owned their own business and been involved with the real estate industry. Since I grew up around office, warehouse and other types of investments, commercial real estate as an alternative asset class never really resonated with me.

As soon as I turned 16, my parents generously bought me a car. But the following Saturday, car keys in hand, I was tasked with meeting contractors and waiting for a plumber at a rental house. I also had to deliver documents to title companies all over town, which — given that this was during the pre-smartphone era — was frustrating. That said, I learned a lot about the nuances of managing real estate, and eventually, this led to my career as a real estate attorney.

I knew that I wanted to do something with real estate, but I was particularly driven by a desire to help people navigate the commercial real estate contract process and minutiae of real estate law.

Five years ago, I opened my own law practice in Dallas, Texas, where I work on a nationwide basis. I feel fortunate to have built a successful practice that allows me to help investors understand commercial real estate law and maximize their returns on investment (ROI).

In writing this book, my goal is to help people who are looking to invest in the industrial and warehouse asset class for the first or second time. Whether it's someone who has already made several commercial investments in other asset classes, or someone who is altogether new to commercial real estate, my hope is that they learn something valuable from this book.

CHAPTER 1

COMMERCIAL AND INDUSTRIAL REAL ESTATE: THE BASICS

Commercial real estate can be defined in many ways, but simply put, it is any type of property primarily owned to generate income. In contrast, residential property is owned primarily for occupancy. For example, a single-family house would be considered residential real estate, even if the owner is renting it out and therefore generating income from it. Real estate is not considered 'commercial' real estate until it reaches a certain scale. For instance, office buildings, warehouses that store shipping goods, and apartment buildings (i.e., multi-family properties) are examples of commercial real estate. Office, hotels, and retail shopping centers are also considered commercial property.

The industrial sector includes warehousing, as well as light manufacturing uses and heavy manufacturing uses with three-phase or four-phase power. A heavy manufacturing industrial building might have rail lines running through the property, multiple overhead cranes, and other types of heavy equipment, whereas a light manufacturing industrial building might just be a warehouse that holds clean, packaged goods.

Investing in Industrial and Warehouse Real Estate

Personally, I am an investor in commercial real estate—specifically industrial and warehouse real estate. I own a couple of buildings around Dallas/Fort Worth, and managing them has taught me a lot about what it's like to actually be an investor and own properties. I am very bullish on this asset class, just from the macroeconomics alone. Through COVID-19, the demand for shipping and warehousing space has increased as more people have been buying and ordering goods online. I believe that the increased penetration of online shipping is going to lead to a permanent increase in demand for all types of warehouse.

The general thesis for industrial and warehouse is that the population is going to continue to grow, and a percentage of the population is going to continue to order and fulfill goods online with a decline of retail space. For every square foot of retail lost, three square feet of warehouse is needed in order to compensate for it.

For anyone who agrees that the demand for online goods will continue, industrial and warehouse real estate represents an outsized return in the commercial real estate market.

The process for determining which asset class or submarket to invest in is always the same, although investment goals and results will differ. I will recommend industrial to an investor who wants a stable place to earn five to eleven percent cash on cash return, and a 25 to 30 percent internal rate of return (IRR) upon exit, long leases with strong credit tenants, and rent increases over time. This investment strategy doesn't require a lot of decision-making, capital improvements, or risk-taking in the interim, which is why I often recommend industrial to this type of investor. For investors who want to complete a transaction in two years and make more money, other solutions within commercial real estate may help them achieve those goals.

CHAPTER 2

IDENTIFYING INVESTOR GOALS AND UNDERSTANDING INDUSTRIAL PROPERTY TYPES

An important question that I ask my clients is, "Where do you see yourself in five years?" In order to answer this question, the investor needs to be able to answer the personal, highly specific, and even somewhat philosophical question of, "What are your goals?"

For an investor, identifying their goals and knowing what they are willing to risk in order to obtain those goals is half the battle. An investor's goals will depend on their circumstances, such as whether they have experience in real estate investment, support a family, or hold a day job, business, or are reliant on other income sources. Answering these questions will help the investor determine how much capital and equity they can risk by investing in a particular property.

In addition, the investor will need to consider their timeframe for repayment of capital, their management goals (e.g., self-management vs. paid property manager), how soon they want to exit, and how much money they want to make.

If the investor's goals are to quickly accumulate and build wealth within two to three years, then they are going to have to take the highest amount of risk with their capital. This might mean buying a vacant building, improving that building, placing a high-quality tenant, and then selling the building.

In terms of purchasing existing buildings (not new development), placing tenants into vacant buildings is the highest ROI for the investor's time and equity; it produces outsized gains for the time and capital invested compared to any other industrial investment.

Once the investor's goals are identified, the investor will have a better idea of how much leverage they can apply when choosing a purchase price. For example, with a down payment of between 20 and 30 percent, and $200,000 to invest, the investor would have a loan in the amount of $800,000, which means they could purchase a $1 million property.

Working backwards from the total purchase price, the investor can look at available commercial properties to determine which fit their goals.

Choosing an Industrial Property Type

There are certain features of a building that determine how heavy of a use it can handle. Some of these features include ceiling height, clear height, dock high doors, and percentage of office space.

Clear height is a driver when it comes to choosing an industrial property type, and it's also a proxy for other parameters of a property. Within all types of commercial real estate, there are the general categories of Class A, Class B, and Class C.

For industrial, a Class A property is going to have very tall clear heights. The clear height may be the highest point in the building, but that may not be the door height, nor the lowest interior height.

Clear height is an important indicator of the amount of goods a tenant could potentially stack in a facility. Some of the newest buildings have a clear height of 30 feet or more, which allows sophisticated tenants to have complex equipment that can stack goods stored at the top of 30-foot racks.

Clear height exists in conjunction with the size of a building. In other words, there probably won't be a 30-foot clear height paired with a 10,000 square-foot building. The caveat to this is that in some cities, such as Seattle or New York City, there are small yet very tall buildings. In most places, a building with a 30-foot clear height will be 100,000 square feet or more. A Class A building with very tall clear heights will not sell for less than about $50 million.

A Class B property will have a clear height of anywhere between 18 and 25 feet, which would pair well with about 50,000 square feet. A building of this size, depending on the tenant, would sell for between $20 and $50 million (circa 2021).

A Class C property will have a clear height of 14 to 16 feet, and is likely to be a much older building (e.g., from the 1960s). It may not have large entry doors and there may be limited door access without multiple loading points, which would limit the use of the interior space. The Class C property is going to command lower rents, which is going to generate a lower net operating income.

Flex buildings are typically one story with a lower clear height and a significant portion of office space, and are very common. A flex tenant may be a church with a three-year lease, which is not necessarily a short lease, but also isn't as long as other industrial leases (e.g., five to 10 years). There are a lot of church tenants that are available for flex office buildings.

Understanding different property types and tenants will help an investor determine which industrial property type best suits their goals. Is the investor willing to work with a broker to find a constant supply of new tenants for a flex building? If so, the investor will be able to earn a higher return, because these buildings might trade at a seven or eight cap versus a Class A, fully occupied single-tenant building, which trades with a five percent cap rate. These are some of the questions that an investor will need to carefully consider when choosing a property type that is most likely to meet their goals.

Important Considerations Prior to Commercial Industrial Investment

The major considerations that need to be made prior to investing in commercial industrial and warehouse real estate include the time involved in pre-acquisition, the reduced commitment during operations, and the financial commitment and liability as it relates to the government, city, and/or tenants.

Pre-Due Diligence

During pre-due diligence research, the investor needs to identify their market and submarket, evaluate the demand for the type of product at hand, and analyze the tenant's use. Understanding the tenant is an important part of being a good landlord and investor. The more research and information on the tenant or potential tenants, the greater the understanding of the property's value and risk.

This research should be done on every single property an investor looks at, but it doesn't mean the investor should buy every single property they look at. For this reason, there's a higher research-to-close ratio or research-to-offer ratio with commercial real estate investments than there is with other types of investments.

Time, Money, and Energy Commitment

All aspects of commercial real estate investment require a greater time, money, and energy commitment than residential or multi family. The time needed to research, underwrite, and properly vet a pre-investment results in higher costs; the investor has to check more boxes, complete the pre-approval process with the lender, and research, interview, and hire a team of professionals, all of which takes effort and time (and for an investor, time is money). However, once you've established your system, the deal size in commercial allows for greater capital deployment per project and a higher return on investor time.

The hold period on commercial real estate is also going to be longer than residential or multi family, because this type of property cannot be sold as quickly or easily as a residential investment, even if it is being sold at a discount.

The entry cost for a smaller building is usually a one to three million dollars. The down payments are going to be much higher (both as a percentage and in absolute terms), especially if the investor is going to be buying a building with vacancies. Lenders will want to see that the investor has cash reserves above and beyond the down payment, because repairs on a commercial property cost significantly more than repairs on a residential property (e.g., a new roof for a commercial property will cost about $100,00, whereas a new roof for a residential property will cost about $10,000). In addition, the time needed to let an industrial property will be longer than other types of asset classes.

Risks

Since commercial real estate investments deal with people's livelihoods (e.g., a tenant's business), tenants are going to insist on accurate and precise lease terms and are not going to be afraid to exert their powers within the lease. For example, if the investor is failing to maintain the parking lot and the lease contains a provision which allows the tenant to resurface or repair the parking lot and charge the investor, then the investor is going to be on the hook for that cost.

In other words, if the investor does not diligently act to repair that obligation, then the tenant is going to do it and incur a fee that will probably be two or three times what it would have cost the investor had they taken the initiative to have the repairs done. These costs will be billed back to the investor in the form of an offset of rent or an invoice.

Benefits

The investor should conclude that the benefits of a commercial industrial investment outweigh the drawbacks and risks. To be clear, there are definitely benefits to investing in commercial industrial and warehouse real estate. For instance, the returns from investing a significant amount of money are going to be much higher than they would be for someone who is trying to assemble a portfolio of single-family rentals.

I love reading about sales and win opportunities, where people find a vacant building that's been sitting for years and needs improvement, and buy it for $30 to $50 per square foot. Once they have the repairs done and get a warranty, they have a great building that national credit tenants will want. They can flip it for $150 per foot, and pocket a few million dollars within two years.

That this can be done is a testament to how much money an investor can make, assuming they are willing to take on the risk of buying a building that's been vacant for years. The bottom line is that a tripling of equity of $2 million per year is pretty good for most investors.

Again, the investor needs to identify the benefits they want (e.g., tax, capital gains, cash flow from income), and be willing to take on the risks in order to obtain them.

CHAPTER 3

THE NINE-STEP LIFE CYCLE OF A COMMERCIAL REAL ESTATE INVESTMENT

1. The life cycle for a commercial real estate investment begins by finding a market. This can start at the state level (e.g., is west coast preferred over Texas?), and then a submarket can be identified. At that point, the investor should determine their desired asset type and goals (e.g., what type of returns they want, what they want to achieve with their time and money).

2. The second step would be to reach out to a lender, this could be through a mortgage broker or directly with a local bank to determine qualifications, interest rates for the chosen submarket, asset type, and loan amount, and the cost of financing.

3. Once the underwriting has been completed and there is a property that fits within the investor's goals, the investor will submit a one to two-page letter of intent (LOI). The more information that is included in that letter, the faster it will align the parties. However, the letter should be completed quickly, because speed is necessary to win deals in the current industrial market.

4. The fourth step is to sign the binding purchase and sale agreement (PSA), open escrow, and deposit the earnest money. The seller will then provide due diligence within the prescribed time.

'Within the prescribed time' is an important term to pay attention to, because many people assume that it will happen on day one. In reality, it depends on what the PSA states; some PSAs have a 15 day period on a 30-day due diligence period to provide all of the documents, which effectively cuts the review time in half. This means that if an investor doesn't have a document in their possession, they are expected to review and make a decision within 15 days.

This situation can differ greatly compared to a situation wherein an attorney is involved and points out that the PSA states that the due diligence should be provided to the buyer within three days. This would result in the buyer having an additional 12 days of review time, which would likely mean feeling more confident moving forward or choosing to renegotiate a particular issue.

There is a broad range of due diligence items that can be ordered, such as an appraisal, property condition report, and Phase 1 Environmental report. This decision-making process can be done with a broker, but an attorney is better suited to provide advice on what is and is not needed for a particular property based on compliance with the lender's requirements.

5. Assuming everything is clear and the loan is approved, the buyer will fund the balance of the purchase price and close on the property.

6. The investor will need to transition tenants, which may involve reviewing a property management contract, or in the case of self-management, using the investor's own paperwork and reviewing the tenants' leases to ensure there is proper assignment, etc.

7. The seventh step is for the investor to implement their plan, whether it is to raise rents, make capital improvements to bring in new tenants, or simply collect rent and maintain the property as is.

8. Next, the investor will prepare their property for sale, which can take anywhere from six to 24

months, depending on the degree to which the investor wants to improve their financials, whether or not they want to re-sign particular tenants to longer leases, etc.

Part of this preparation should involve consulting an attorney about tax strategies, how to deal with the proceeds and/or capital gains, and the various tax options available to them.

Ultimately, the investor can sell at a price that their broker recommends or at a price that they are comfortable with, given the market.

9. Rinse and repeat until the investor has met all of their goals. This traditional cycle is applicable to any type of commercial real estate, not just industrial.

CHAPTER 4

TRANSITIONING FROM RESIDENTIAL TO COMMERCIAL REAL ESTATE INVESTMENTS

There is a fair number of people who invest in residential real estate before moving on to commercial real estate, but I wouldn't say it's a majority. For those who do make this transition, the motivation is usually about scale. To elaborate, if someone is looking at a single-family portfolio spread out or clustered, then they'll have eight of everything to deal with, like roofs, washers and dryers, refrigerators, sewer mains, and electrical lines. To put it simply, this can amount to all an inordinate amount of focus, time and energy to solve multiples of each problem.

Speaking from personal experience, when I was dealing with five to six units, something was always breaking on one property or another, leaving me with the responsibility of making decisions about how to allocate resources (e.g., whether to or how much to spend for a new appliance). While the property manager can make some of these decisions, they will still ask the investor a lot of questions. And when something goes wrong every single month, it can be frustrating to have to answer the questions over and over.

For all of these reasons, the issue of scale is what drives most people to transition to commercial real estate investments. If an investor were to consolidate all of the equity from multiple single-family properties and put it into one or two commercial properties, the number of monthly problems would decrease, while the impact or magnitude of each problem would increase. Commercial real estate problems may be more costly, but investors now have the benefit of guidance from paid professionals which makes all the difference.

To Transition or to Not Transition?

The decision to transition from residential to commercial real estate investing requires an analysis by the investor themselves, especially with regard to the amount of time they have available. If real estate investing is not their full-time job, they need to be aware of the significant (but uneven) time investment required. The following are also important considerations:

- **Responsiveness and Preparedness**

In the commercial world of real estate, an investor's responsiveness has to be aligned with the industry in order to win deals, partners, vendors, and tenants. In contrast, the residential real estate world offers some leeway in terms of timeliness and responsiveness to non-critical issues. Letting a problem sit for a several weeks in the commercial world just isn't acceptable to commercial tenants, and people won't want to work with an investor who has a reputation for doing this.

The investor will need to pay bills, respond to quotes, and address matters promptly. This means that the commercial real estate investor needs to have a proactive team in place, and enough time to properly manage their investment properties.

- **Money Shouldn't Be an Issue**

When it comes to the decision of whether to transition from residential to commercial real estate investments, cost is much less of an issue. If an investor has a good deal on their hands and the metrics work, there is always money; in fact, there is more money than there are deals.

Even with only one commercial deal per year, the investor is going to make more money than they would on a residential property, simply because of the amount of capital deployed versus the time to underwrite. This will remain true as the investor's time grows more valuable with increased investment knowledge.

As an investor's time becomes more valuable, they will want to earn a commensurate return for their time. For instance, with a 40,000 square-foot building, the time invested as a principal is likely to be about twice as much as time invested for a SFR, but the return will be 400 percent more than any residential property.

- **Vacancy Risk**

Vacancy risk poses the biggest threat to annual cash flow, but also be mitigated by having a multi-tenant property or reduced mortgage payments (if any). For example, a multi-bay warehouse and four or five tenants that are roughly equal, the investor would be able to withstand 40%vacancy while maintaining revenue to cover fixed expenses: principal and interest payment, property taxes, repairs, etc. Having multiple tenants compared to a single tenant in a single unit is a very useful hedge against vacancy risk.

- **Have Some Humility**

When transitioning from residential property investments to commercial property investments, a certain amount of humility is helpful, if not necessary. Even if the investor has been successful with one type of asset class, they need to understand that that there is going to be a learning curve.

To be successful, an investor needs to be open to learning from others, and in order to truly learn from others, there has to be some level of humility. The investor might choose to work with a team that has experience in the market at hand, rather than assume that simply because they successfully handled a multi-family property, they can handle a warehouse.

- **Important Differences**

Two of the main differences between residential properties and commercial properties are the tenants and the physical plan of the buildings. To be successful, an investor to needs to understand these differences. For example, if an investor is coming from a multi-family property, then they will be accustomed to dealing with standardized form leases, often with gross payment terms (landlord that pays all taxes, utilities, maintenance, lawncare, snow removal, etc.) that are often promulgated by a state agency or a private organization. As a result, most leases on a multi family building will be identical causing investors to disregard lease review as an important part of due diligence.

In contrast, there is really no such thing as a 'standard' commercial industrial lease; an investor who decides to transition to commercial property investments will be dealing with custom-drafted leases. Nearly every tenant is going to make changes, even if the landlord puts out their form. Failing to look at the lease closely could mean overlooking a termination clause, which could be very detrimental to the value and the cash flow of the building. Of course, there are lesser clauses that are less catastrophic, but nonetheless impactful. Investors should never assume that reading one lease is sufficient, because each lease could differ in a number of ways. This could set up an investor for a shock when, a couple of years after acquisition, a tenant exercises their early termination right, of which the investor was unaware. The bottom line is this: for an industrial property, every single tenant lease should be reviewed.

CHAPTER 5

BROKERS VS. ATTORNEYS

The broker's primary job is to advise on the market, purchase price, lease business terms, tenancy prospects, and rates per square foot. Have a question about the cost of a new overhead door? The answer would be outside of the broker's wheelhouse.

The attorney's primary job is to ensure that the Purchase and Sale Agreement (PSA), lease agreements, and title/survey represent what the client understands they are buying. This often involves reviewing and revising the language and making changes to phrases, clauses, and entire sentences or paragraphs—none of which is in the broker's wheelhouse.

The out-of-state investor is likely to be working with a broker, but it's important to remember that a broker is only getting paid on contingency, which means brokers have a natural incentive to close deals no matter what. In other words, the broker's interests differ slightly from the investor's interests. A broker is likely to encourage the investor to close a deal so that they themselves can get paid.

An attorney, on the other hand, gets paid regardless of whether the property closes, and will always have the investor's best interests in mind. As a fiduciary, an attorney owes a duty to each and every client, which creates alignment between the lawyer and the client.

If an investor is not in the market on a day-to-day basis, then they will only be hearing the opinion of the broker, and it's difficult to make a decision based only on one data point. Bringing in a lawyer means bringing in a second data point, which is essential for anyone who is making these types of decisions.

If the investor does not understand something in the contract, they can't turn to the broker because the broker cannot provide legal advice; the investor will have to ask a lawyer. This brings to light the primary tension between brokers and attorneys, which is that brokers will give their opinion based on their experience and even write longer amendments that introduce more ambiguity than clarity.

For instance, a broker might add language which extends the closing date by five days; on its face, this may be fine, but as an attorney, I would specify whether those five days are calendar days or business days, and what happens if one of those five days falls on a holiday. There are all sorts of legal additions that an attorney might draft in order to make a contract more precise, and thereby cover all bases in the event that there is a disagreement about performance.

Legally, an investor in Texas is not required to hire a broker nor an attorney; there is nothing prohibiting them from submitting and reviewing their own contract, determining a price, and buying a property. Certainly, this has been done in the past and will continue in the future. That said, the new investors don't know what they don't know if it's the investor's first time purchasing commercial property.

When dealing with a new investor, find a law firm willing to walk you through the process from start to finish. Ask them for checklists, calendar deadlines, document turnaround expectations, and what they expect from the client in terms of communication. Once an investor has gone through the process once, you can make your own decisions about which professionals to hire on a second purchase. Without having questions answered at least once from an attorney, it is impossible for an investor to know what it takes to do it right, and whether they could benefit from the guidance of an attorney in future transactions.

CHAPTER 6

THE IMPORTANCE OF HIRING LEGAL COUNSEL

An attorney can help in many ways, such as with the due diligence process, finding a market, finding a specific property, submitting letters of intent, transitioning tenants, and obtaining, applying for, and reviewing loan documents.

Commercial real estate investors are a brave people who set out on a journey, putting real money and hard-earned equity at risk without any guaranteed return. The attorney, is a guide to show them how to climb the mountain and not just point out all the ways it could potentially go wrong.

Investors need to make sure they're aware of the potential risks, but building a team focused on guiding them on the path forward, and provide solutions that align with the investor's goals. As an attorney and an industrial investor myself, I come from a place of education, legal expertise, and personal investment experience.

Large private-equity firms like Prologis, Brookfield, and Blackstone understand the risks of commercial real estate investments; they've done more transactions than anyone out there, yet they are still hiring legal counsel. Large equity groups that don't have outside counsel have full-time in-house counsel, so they always have someone who can answer their legal questions.

Why is it that even these large, experienced firms rely on legal counsel? It's because they understand the risks.

Most investors who believe they can handle the entire commercial real estate investment process by themselves underestimate the risk or have not been involved in a costly lawsuit yet. It never makes sense for a commercial real estate investor to do everything themselves. Instead learning how to leverage your time and strengths will create a professional team needed to become a successful investor.

When an Attorney Should Get Involved

Ideally, a law firm should get involved with an industrial or warehouse commercial real estate transaction as early as possible. Not hiring a commercial broker is one reason to bring on an attorney, but there tend to be natural points during the process when an attorney is brought in for assistance. For example, it may be when letters of intent need to be submitted, the PSA needs to be negotiated, or questions about an LLC or structuring partnership agreements need to be answered.

A common oversight occurs when an attorney is not working on a case has to do with the scope of seller representations. A property being sold 'as is' doesn't necessarily mean that the property has no warranties. For example, if the seller has included disclaimers on an electrical system, stating that it is being sold as is, the investor can add language which makes the owner liable in the event that the electrical system violates or is in some way noncompliant with the code. Without adding this condition, the investor could find themselves with a $30,000 bill and the need to rewire the entire electrical service panel.

It's important to note that once the PSA has been executed, the parties are locked in. For this reason, an attorney should be consulted during the pre-signing stage. While an attorney can still provide value throughout the acquisition process, even if they were hired after the signing of the PSA, it does weaken the attorney's ability to advocate on the client's behalf in terms of representations, warranties, and due diligence concerns.

Once a contract has been signed, there is a limited amount of room for adjustments and negotiations, and in most cases, it's possible to terminate and receive the earnest money back. However, investors should know that in the commercial real estate market, reputation matters — a lot. If an investor is perceived as re-trading a deal, their reputation will be hurt and fewer people will want to work with them in the future. An investor who wants to make adjustments or terminate a contract once it's been signed and who also wants to maintain a good reputation should have a solid justification, such as an assumption that turned out to be false.

Searching for a Good Real Estate Lawyer

There are certain questions that all clients should ask of potential professional service providers, whether it's a certified public accountant (CPA), broker, lawyer, insurance agent, or anyone else with whom the investor is working. By using a standard set of questions, the client can compare responses from different service providers.

The first time someone meets with a lawyer, it should be in a face-to-face environment if it cannot be in person (e.g., video conference). At Ronald Rohde

Law, we often use video conferencing and find it to be an immediate way of interacting with potential clients. During the first meeting, the client should ask the lawyer to tell them about their firm and legal experience, as this information will provide the client with insight as to whether the attorney is capable of helping them meet their goals.

If an attorney doesn't have experience handling a particular property subtype that the investor is looking to purchase (e.g., a five-story mini storage with automated elevators), that wouldn't necessarily be just cause to disqualify them as an option, so long as the attorney has handled mini or RV storage buildings in the past and has worked within the same city. That said, the client should ask questions about the particular submarket and property subtype that they are interested in purchasing.

The client should also ask the attorney about their fees. It is my belief that attorneys should be transparent about when and how costs are incurred so that the client has a clear picture of what to expect.

Yet another important question to ask is how the attorney tends to communicate with their clients, such as by phone, email, and/or text. If the client prefers a particular form of communication, they should ask whether the attorney can accommodate that.

Finally, the client should ask the attorney about their idea of the ideal client and non-ideal client. This tends to be a hard question to answer, but it is very useful for clients to know what a non-ideal client looks like.

Ronald Rohde Law

Much of the work at Ronald Rohde Law is done in Texas, where we are very familiar with the state laws and local customs. However, we can perform all of our functions nearly nationwide. If there is a local state law issue, then we can bring in local counsel.

At Ronald Rohde Law, we are happy to tell people when something is outside of our wheelhouse and when it isn't a good fit. Clients appreciate when service providers know what they do well, because they can't necessarily do everything well. That said, we offer a number of services, including contract review, title commitment/survey review, and lease reviews.

The key service produce that we provide are drafting and negotiating purchase and sale contracts and reviewing due diligence documents. To the extent that a commercial investment relies on the property acquired, the strength of the tenant lease is critical to the entire transaction. If you are buying the streams of future income, then you are buying the lease agreement.

INDEX

NOTES